ABSTRACTIONS

Other Recent Work anthologies:
Metamorphic: 21st century poets respond to Ovid
Poet to Poet: Contemporary women poets from Japan
Cities: 10 poets, 10 cities
5,6,7,8
Tract: Prose poems
Pulse: Prose poems
Seam: Prose poems

ABSTRACTIONS

edited by Paul Munden and Shane Strange

RECENT
WORK
PRESS

Abstractions
Recent Work Press
Canberra, Australia

Copyright © the authors, 2018

ISBN: 9780648257998 (paperback)

 A catalogue record for this book is available from the National Library of Australia

All rights reserved. This book is copyright. Except for private study, research, criticism or reviews as permitted under the Copyright Act, no part of this book may be reproduced, stored in a retrieval system, or transmitted in any form by any means without prior written permission. Enquiries should be addressed to the publisher.

Cover photograph: © Fiona Edmonds Dobrijevich, 2017
Cover design: Recent Work Press
Set by Recent Work Press

recentworkpress.com

CONTENTS

INTRODUCTION i
Paul Munden and Shane Strange

CONJECTURE
After empathy   3
Andy Jackson
Andachtsbilder   4
Shane Strange
Painting   6
Paul Hetherington
If we take   7
Vahni Capildeo
Tripping over koans   8
Jen Webb
Cold case   9
John Foulcher
What if risk   10
Paul Munden
What Bill Murray might have whispered to Scarlett Johansson in the farewell scene of *Lost in Translation*   11
Melinda Smith
this poem is silenced against its will   13
Monica Carroll
Dream   14
Katharine Coles

OBLIGATION
Hold your arm like a branch   17
Vahni Capildeo

Newcastle reckoning	18
Melinda Smith	
Mother poem	20
Katharine Coles	
Mutual obligation	21
Andy Jackson	
Amphibian	22
John Foulcher	
Woman and man	23
Paul Hetherington	
The music lesson	24
Jen Webb	
King's Canyon	25
Paul Munden	
Things you get fucked with	26
Monica Carroll	
Portrait of the Queensland police officer as a young man	27
Shane Strange	

NONSENSE

Instructions for use of hands	31
John Foulcher	
Where the March Hare runs	32
Paul Hetherington	
After Martin Carter, 'This is the Dark Time, My Love'	33
Vahni Capildeo	
Gone fishing	34
Paul Munden	
Some assembly required	35
Melinda Smith	

No reason	37
Katharine Coles	
When myth turns to truth	38
Jen Webb	
Knuckle down	39
Monica Carroll	
Saru, the monkey god, describes a laundromat in Kyoto	40
Shane Strange	
In your language	41
Andy Jackson	

SPACE

Space	45
Paul Hetherington	
Erasure after William Empson's 'Aubade' (1)	46
Vahni Capildeo	
The silent builders	47
John Foulcher	
red, white and window	48
Melinda Smith	
forbid the cleaving rumours	49
Monica Carroll	
Beyond the walls	50
Jen Webb	
Flight	51
Shane Strange	
Instructions for client restraint	52
Andy Jackson	
Floor plan	53
Katharine Coles	

'Road closed' 54
Paul Munden

PLEASURE

Apes rule 59
Melinda Smith
He marvels 60
Paul Munden
Organ recital 61
Katharine Coles
There are many pleasures 62
Andy Jackson
So far, she's missing 63
Vahni Capildeo
Surfing the waves 64
Jen Webb
This is what it feels like 65
Monica Carroll
Through eye-gate, and ear-gate into the city of child-soul 66
Shane Strange
Gathering 67
Paul Hetherington
On pleasure 68
John Foulcher

IDENTITY

On a carefree afternoon such as this 71
Paul Munden
Thought experiment 72
Monica Carroll

Bloodnut gut-wrench   73
   Melinda Smith
Epistemology   74
   John Foulcher
Beauty, from the other side   75
   Andy Jackson
Methods for the identification of individuals, living or dead   77
   Shane Strange
The man in the street   78
   Paul Hetherington
Scaling the walls   79
   Jen Webb
Dog tag   80
   Katharine Coles
Hear her relax release   81
   Vahni Capildeo

RHYTHM

If there were five people   85
   Monica Carroll
Lines from an ECG   86
   Andy Jackson
Once more with feeling   87
   Shane Strange
A summer in the tundra   88
   Jen Webb
Accidental   89
   Katharine Coles
Beating the mix   90
   John Foulcher

After Sir Philip Sidney, *Astrophil and Stella* 31   91
   Vahni Capildeo
Jazz quartet   92
   Melinda Smith
With daily practice   94
   Paul Munden
Syncopation   95
   Paul Hetherington

ACCURACY

A very small history of reading   99
   Shane Strange
What do you mean by 'fake'?   100
   Katharine Coles
Marks   101
   Melinda Smith
Clockwork   105
   Paul Munden
Quiver   107
   Paul Hetherington
By the river of   108
   Monica Carroll
An atheist for God   109
   John Foulcher
Erasure after William Empson's 'Aubade' (2)   110
   Vahni Capildeo
No relief maps   111
   Andy Jackson
The cartographer   112
   Jen Webb

COST

National museum of women in the arts   115
  Katharine Coles
Human looking   116
  Andy Jackson
When he charged   118
  Paul Munden
The driveway   119
  John Foulcher
Handwritten   120
  Paul Hetherington
Cyclone season   121
  Jen Webb
The road to Pac Bo   122
  Shane Strange
My tiny hippopotamus   123
  Vahni Capildeo
DIY empire   124
  Melinda Smith
Questions for the knife   125
  Monica Carroll

YOUTH

So many roads to go   129
  Jen Webb
Bruise   130
  Paul Hetherington
That photo   131
  Andy Jackson
Deportment   132
  Katharine Coles

Advice poetry   133
Shane Strange
The band   135
John Foulcher
Their father still refused   136
Paul Munden
As we rolled out the tape measure tongue   137
Monica Carroll
every each day best   138
Vahni Capildeo
Interrupting the bread-making   139
Melinda Smith

NOTES   141
BIOGRAPHIES   142

INTRODUCTION

1.

Ok poets, we get it. Things are like other things.

This meme came up in one of our social media feeds last year. Like the best examples of our new media culture, it is pithy and apposite, wryly reducing the complex historical and global act of making, listening, reading and performing poetry to 10 words that speak, with an inescapable logic, to poetry's central purpose as a representational art form. 'But poetry is so much more than that!' an internal voice protests. 'No... it isn't,' comes the bemused reply.

The word 'abstraction' derives from the Latin *abstrahere* 'to draw away from'. Often, when we think of the concept of abstraction, we perceive it negatively: as a form of removal from the practical or the quotidian, an opposite to lived experience and the sensuous details of the world; or, as in the meme above, a kind of reduction of complexity into simpler concepts. Abstraction is, in this sense, an ideal process, removed from the concrete through thought.

But abstraction is also a power. We are surrounded by abstractions, ruled by them: money, time, love, morality, language (is language an abstraction?). Where do abstractions begin? Do they arise from experience, or shape it? Or both? Although immaterial they can be, nonetheless, all too real. Abstractions, then, aren't merely a 'drawing away from' but also a conceptual and material 'moving towards'.

Poetry is in a beautiful bind here, stuck in a desire to make 'things like other things', to allude to, or confuse, or open out a perceived essence or commonality. And yet it often does so in a personal, experiential, and sensuous way. In Thomas Hardy's first published novel, *Desperate Remedies*, he describes character Ambrose Graye as having 'a quality of thought which, exercised on homeliness, was humour; on nature, picturesqueness; on abstractions, poetry.' Poetry here is a 'heightened' form of abstraction, a transformative capacity, a mark, in Hardy's view, of distinction.

With the onset of modernism, abstraction is something we are warned against. Before he began spruiking for Mussolini, Ezra Pound told us to '[g]o in fear of abstractions', since 'the natural object is always the *adequate* symbol'[1], while William Carlos Williams famously suggests 'no ideas but in things.' A favourite creative writing mantra is 'show don't tell,' to use the concrete to allude to but never name an abstract concept. US poet Ravi Shankar suggests:

> *This bias toward the materiality, not of language, but rather of the world as represented in language, is lodged so deeply in the poetic psyche that a poem laden with abstractions can almost be considered a de facto failure.*[2]

However, it is also through and beyond modernism that we begin to see those great abstract movements in all art forms, exemplified by diverse practices such as Dadaism, Language poetry and varying concrete, conceptual and experimental poetry practices, which utilise abstractions up to and beyond the limits of strictly representational form. Poetry under this influence is freed from having to 'mean' and language's seemingly transparent connection to the material world is deconstructed and problematised, foregrounding, and making a virtue of, its opaque connection to the tangible and the real.

2.

So, what made us come up with an anthology whose guiding principle was the slippery slope of abstraction? Part of our mission at Recent Work Press is to produce a range of collaborative poetry anthologies that set 'challenges' for the poets involved with a view to seeing what happens. Having just released the *Cities* anthology in 2017, we were working in adjacent offices at the University of Canberra, deciding what might work for another anthology of this type, when the idea of abstraction was put forward. It was enticing. What if we ignored the modernists' call to the concrete, 'the thing', and went straight for the abstract concept—getting, in some sense, to the heart of the matter? This seemed like an interesting experiment, but what abstractions

---

1 Pound, E 'A few don'ts from an Imagiste' 1913 *Poetry Magazine*
2 Shankar R 'In praise of abstraction: Moving beyond concrete imagery' 2005 *poets.org* https://www.poets.org/poetsorg/text/praise-abstraction-moving-beyond-concrete-imagery

would we use? The usual suspects arose—love, justice, death, money—but these seemed to be well covered in the poetic tradition, and, to be honest, not particularly engaging in their raw form. Perhaps modernist sensibilities still tugged at our sleeves. We had to arrive at abstractions that intrigued the poets involved, presenting them with problems to be solved, but were neither conceptually obscure nor blindingly obvious. In this we came across the problem of what might or might not be considered an abstraction. Was this or that abstract enough? What exactly did we mean by abstract? Isn't everything in language an abstraction?

Eventually, after many lists of words, and an increasing sense of falling down a rabbit hole from which we would never emerge, we found a way of settling on 10 abstract concepts for 10 very real poets. The anthology you have before you presents 100 poems: responses to each of the abstractions from each of the poets.

We also wanted our abstractions to steer a line between the political and the poetic, the social and the personal, to be provocations as well as spurs to composing poetry. And this, we think, can be seen clearly in the results. Whether reflecting on gender politics, the current political situation in the US, the vicissitudes of disability under neoliberalism, the financial climate, or police brutality; or the roles of memory and history, art and love, music and science, in everyday experience or over the course of a life, the poems in this book do more than ample justice to our conceit. In many ways they have exceeded it. The variety of form is also notable, suggesting that the conceptual challenge also pushed some poets very profitably into new structural territory.

We should like to thank all the poets who joined us in the exercise for engaging willingly and fully in our project, with generosity and good humour.

Paul Munden and Shane Strange

CONJECTURE

After empathy

a double acrostic

clambering out of my bones into your skin, this
optimistic *what if,* this bodily dressing-up with
no harm meant, I don't expect the entry to be so
jarring—rattled and adrift in the loose fit of you,
every attempt to grasp something solid fails, until
confidence dissolves in the acid of your gut, and
this is what I'm left with—the visceral trouble of
undoing what I've assumed—drenched in you, a
road slowly opening in the human dark, at last I
emerge, dumbstruck, my entire body an ear, still

Andy Jackson

Andachtsbilder

1. *A fisherman's coat is an oilskin*

   My son the angel:
   oblivious to wisdom,
   awkward as a seismograph,
   slips into my mistakes
   like a new coat.

2. *After an earthquake help others if you are able*

   In his bedroom everything
   is as he left it:
   the clothes in the wardrobe,
   the books in a line
   on the shelf. I feel
   the not him keenly.

3. *At the hospital we line up like penitents*

   At each station I recite
   'Do not let my son die.'
   I hear back the sound
   of the ocean,
   or is it nothing?

4. *Seagulls are one of the few animals that can drink salt water*

   Do we know,
   or do we stop ourselves from knowing
   what is to come?
   At the monastery
   a pensive Christ thinks
   'What if I'd stuck
   to carpentry?'

5. *The sea in this poem represents the vast unknown*

> Last night I watched the ocean
> nail its hands to the coastline.
> I thought I saw an angel,
> But it was only a gull.

Shane Strange

Painting

What is that picture 'saying'? We stand, conjecturing; you take my hand; the carriage of years says, 'yes, we know it'. We look again at the man in oil paint addressing the window, the young woman on the chair; we look at each other, sensing we're speculation—like sieves through which we might fall. We see ourselves in a painting, catch each other's eyes. You ask, 'What is the painting saying?' and we nod, knowing that meaning rests between our reaching hands.

Paul Hetherington

If we take

all the fish
out the lake
once a year,
if we check
for native fish
against invasive fish,
if we put
invasive fish in
special boxes, put
native fish back
in the lake,
if we take
good care, use
pure detergents, soap-
free soap, perhaps
the lake will
from its dark
rough clear north
to its green
choppy south be
good to us,
livable, never gentle,
never yet measured,
not cause drowning,
drought, not be
cross, or crossed.

Vahni Capildeo

Tripping over koans

Mountains that once were mountains, rivers that imagine themselves as streams. It's not as though you didn't know this before you sent your GoPro into those sites, but now you have the evidence: bushfires resolving into spirals of suns, bones giving up their plans. That woman you loved who said incomprehensible things: that rivers are not rivers; that the mountain is no mountain—where did she go? Could you possibly find her again? The mountain is there, where it has always been; you have slept every night in its shadow. But today it seems to be dissolving, there where the sunset meets the rock, and the only things that are real are the fire, and your own uncertainty.

Jen Webb

Cold case

In the early hours, we wake to the tune of sirens:
from my window, I can see a woman's body
lying in a pool of dreams. It's not a pretty sight.
Some of her dreams are pure, some are filled
with lust and sweat, and some are as black
as the hour. In one of these, she's eating a man,
picking at his bones. Forensic experts slip
clots of dream into plastic bags and hand them on
to a grim-faced sergeant who whispers *I've seen
some sick things, but this ...* A constable concurs:
Looks to me like suicide. Jesus. What a way to go.

John Foulcher

What if risk

rhymed with happiness, happiness with love? ... he sensed a new poetics in the making, prosody ousted by a bastard calculus, unfathomable to all: art rhymed with science, politics with peace; para-rhymes included halo and holiday, danube and dance; fido and felix were there in the mix—he was thinking, surely, of *fidelity* and *felicity*, but his efforts crumbled to an ad for inferior pet food brands; an algorithm was introduced to handle what was soon called 'future beauty' or 'speculative truth', but when push came to shove there was still a call for—what did they once call it?—a boomerang/slang

Paul Munden

What Bill Murray might have whispered to Scarlett Johansson in the farewell scene of Lost in Translation

Hey you,…

I love it when you look up
    tabun, ne 多分、ね 'probably'
        ('it might be like that, yes, in most cases')

the east is black
    soo rashii desu そうらしいです
        'so it would appear (from what people say)'

the west is a long gold anxiety
    daroo だろう 'probably'

a jade heart, a thousand radiances, gravity
    soo to omowareru そうと思われる
        'you could think of it like that'

you have shed them all
    da soo desu だそうです 'so I hear'

you will be so clean
    to itte mo okashiku wa nai と言ってもおかしくはない
        'you could say that'
        ('even if you said that it wouldn't be strange')

white bolt blue
    soo yuu ki ga suru そういう気がする
        'I have that kind of feeling'

I have to bury what I know
     sono yoo desu　そのようです
         'so it seems (from what I can see)'

this is the wrong miracle
     soo ka mo shirenai　そうかもしれない
         'maybe' ('whether it is or not, we can't know')

…OK, bye

Melinda Smith

this poem is silenced against its will

It is possible that the two Editors of this volume will refuse to publish this work on conjecture citing grounds that it is not a poem. Should this unfortunate incident arise, and this poem is silenced against its will—black electrical tape stretched over the mouth stuffed with dirty rags that stifle screams—please, complete and post the form below.

	Affix stamp here

Recent Work Press
10 Ashby Cct.
Kambah ACT 2902

Dear Paul & Shane

I, the undersigned, object to the patriarchal conservative petrified gagging of all poems, poetry and poem-like structures.

Free the form!

Sincerely

[insert   name_____]

Monica Carroll

Dream

For WC

Outside my friend's window a path

Branches. Down the right fork
He finds an apple tree, twisted and old

As any story, though nothing says

Fairy tale to him. Down the left fork—
But he's never seen the left fork.

The apples are too delicious.

Katharine Coles

OBLIGATION

Hold your arm like a branch,

swaying from the shoulder
solid in a balance
a sitting hawk may trust.
Number the thirteen ducks,
fed with appropriate
proteins, none of your bread,
maybe peanut butter.
Think on such things while you
wait, while they fail to raise
a vein, when the raised vein
is childsize, when they save
on equipment, and won't
change needles. Hold your arm.

Vahni Capildeo

Newcastle reckoning

The Moreton Bay fig trees have received the signal
They are dropping their sticky treasure-bags,
the small coins of seed spill and scatter in dark clumps
I am sitting in a house on a hill, The Hill, sitting
in a pale green chair, high up

in the hot blue air above the estuary, sitting
and being filmed, it is the first time
I have ever been on camera
and known it, the shock and squirm
seeing my own jaw obscenely working, my own

smug cheeks below my vacant eyes
We are filming in a house on a hill, The Hill,
but I do not know its Awabakal name
and I have neither sought nor received
permission to enter here

I am rude and unprotected, jaw working
and working, sitting like a pale green insult
The birds in the fig trees are raucous, they keep
ruining the recording, we have to do take after take
There is an angry man mounting the stairs

from the basement, he is making noises with his mouth
about insurance and preconditions   We do not
comprehend him but it seems we must leave
The smell from the basement is cold
off the convict-hewn sandstone, it is

clammy and cemetery, rotten with loss
We pack up the camera, move on   It is a stifling
afternoon, the breeze keeps failing, my breath
is shallow and I am slick behind the knees
The fallen figs stick to my shoes,

they are trying to tell me something
about preconditions, about the reproductive
cycle of betrayal   As the dusk comes in
I am sleeved with mosquitoes
I want to tell them to leave, but I do not know

their Awabakal names   The half-moon rises,
magnified in the hot air, it knows
I have neither sought nor received permission,
it knows about my people, it has watched them
as they slit the skin of the land upriver, has watched them,

working and working, obscenely
gouging the coal from under her ribs
The birds cry and cry again in the fig-branches,
they are making noises with their bird-mouths
trying to tell me something

about treasure, and small coins, and sandstone;
about memory, shallow and slick   We stop and sit on the steps
halfway down to King St   The old broken-in-half moon,
a headstone, inverted, showing her bone-self, hangs
clammy and cemetery over the asphalt, over Civic Park

over all the unmarked graves   There is an anger
mounting from under the fig-roots, magnified
by each insult   We do not comprehend   It wants us to leave
This air is rotten with loss, but we are still sitting,
and sitting, living on it, breathing it in

Melinda Smith

Mother poem

People are never who we believe.
Why should they be? Especially
When she wields future angles
And gorgeous silver hair. Imagine,

Thirty years on, for example, you
Trailing intellect and charm, real
As the future, so don't let her kid
You. Her evident interest, her side-

Cocked head: she might even be
Listening
            and all that. Meanwhile,
Here in the real, you never will
Escape. If not her, someone

Always remembers what you ate,
Exactly where you sit.

Katharine Coles

Mutual obligation

the institutions hollowed out, you're cornered by an idea of independence
                                      rent-stress and diagnosis
    work, the only rope thrown into the hole

some of those employed do well, seem intact, while others are rushed to
                                emergency missing a limb or a mind
    left with the therapy of paperwork

your body employs you in the labour of bone-pain and flesh-hurt, the
                              small steps through the pharmaceutical minefield
    the work of falling to earth

the tenure of trying to do no harm to yourself, the painstaking translations
                              of the body's murmurs and sparks
    the work of being human

on call to climb precarious impairment tables, to prove just how incapable
                              you are and yet how able and willing
    you do want to work don't you?

still this hacking through forests of symptoms and prescriptions, desperate
                            to lie down in a sunlit clearing, to rest
    to be heard and to be held

in the mutual obligation of shared air, where the work consists of listening
                                to each other's troubled breathing
    with no solution to offer but this

Andy Jackson

Amphibian

When I left school
at last, after forty years,
it was the dream of a sunny Sunday,
the warm air ruffling the grass
like a father ruffling his son's hair
as they walk to his first day in kindergarten,
the paradise of being young
soon to be soured by the toad work.
After forty years, leaving
at last a life of red ink and desks,
I heard something croak in the sun-soaked grass.

John Foulcher

Woman and man

1.

Leaving the painting we move towards another—impasto, a landscape, something modern. Yet we're still drawn to the first, thinking of beauty, holding its image of a woman and man in mind; its close interior spaces. We feel an obligation—to try to see it well; to take it into eyes like an embrace; to search its multiple suggestions. The new painting might be a coastline—lurid orange and red trees clutter the threshold; sand becomes water—an image of what we know and what we don't. You say, 'I must go back'. A sense of holding to what we love; an intimate pact.

2.

You stood on a boat on the Grand Canal and light stitched your hair with yellow. You spoke about paintings, explaining techniques and context, pointing to reproductions on your iPhone. You gestured reverently towards Giorgione's *La Tempesta*, insisting on its strangeness. The canal swerved and a boat coughed towards a mooring. A man disembarked, then a woman and child, as lightning gouged the sky. The old town stood as if to attention. She carried her child like the Madonna of Tenderness; he hoisted baggage as if chivalry inhered in his gestures. 'We have an obligation to the past,' you said, studying an image of Giorgione's masterwork, wishing for 'light, more light.'

Paul Hetherington

The music lesson

He lifts the ney, takes a breath. Half notes and quarter notes spill out, and are caught up by the oud player, and the cellist from across the way who is sitting in just for the moment, and the young man who claws his first braying note back into the garden of this maqam. They push and pull the notes between them, trading string and breath and blow. No one wants to be the first to cry uncle, to give away the sixth note, or the eighth. He stops them. Listen, he says. And shivers through the tonic, then the fifth, then the fourth. Listen, he says again. To play this, you must copy every note; and then with each note, make it new.

Jen Webb

King's Canyon

was a road too far, a fact
that held with what you'd planned—
tempting as it was to veer
recklessly off-course—aware
that what you lacked

was the right companion
with whom to share
the risk of the red land
turning to red river.

Paul Munden

Things you get fucked with

white picket fence
a white picket
anything white

Things you fuck up

ferns antelope zinc bees clouds oceans mud crows hills silica oaks worms kelp sparrows rivers oysters pigeons slopes milkwort argon octopi skinks deserts copper tadpoles wattle clover silt dandelions cranes geckos bark grasslands shade air platypus moss tomato frogs tin huntsmen cuckoos lakes brown bears clay silk worms granite trout sap earwigs rain baboons glaciers crickets rocks sand pipers escarpments musk ox deltas apples temperatures fossils beavers migrations falcons salt turtles streams carbon dingoes salmon prairies termites cobras beech flax red foxes nitrogen reefs sea otters biomes ants firths hares cliffs kingfishers snow gold impala islands puddles fire salamanders mercury dogwood oxygen sand booklice radon sea horse rubber squirrels mountains lyrebirds aquifers sting rays lochs damsels canyons pronghorns ducks yams coal waterfalls flint currents dirt the three sisters

Things that fuck you over are no excuse

See cliché: trial
Follow with: tribulation

You: *Oh shit, I can't handle this*
You in reply to you: *Fuck you*

Don't be a jerk about it. Draw a line. Make clear this gets crossed, you're fucked.

Monica Carroll

Portrait of the Queensland police officer as a young man

To staunch the flow of blood
he would have to reverse the punch
and unhear the 'cunt' addressed to him
from the mouth of the man whose hands
were cuffed behind his back.
And, through a series of re-contortions,
unhandle that man's body and release him
into the back seat of the police car from where he came.
And he would have to watch that car reverse
up the street in front of the lockup
and return to the conversation with his Sergeant
who he would have to unhear saying
'No copper took shit from an abo'.

And returning home he would have to de-dress
and stand, clean in his own skin,
pushing water into the shower's nozzle,
unthinking little affirmations,
re-applying his stubble,
walking backward down the hall,
decompressing muscle,
unfucking his fiancée, and
slide into a coma from where
he would never have to remember.

Shane Strange

NONSENSE

Instructions for use of hands

Her hands are wearing out.
The middle finger on her left hand
has fallen off, neither thumb will clutch.
She fears they will be useless soon.
She hovers over catalogues, finds some hands
on special, fidgets with her credit card
and pays, her fingers crossed. When the hands
arrive, she opens the box with her feet.
The instructions are in English, Mandarin
and Sign. *Some stiffness may be evident*
they say *but this will pass. Take time
to stretch your new hands. Study the nails.
You can customise these. Some people
paint them as red as their genitals,
while others blunt them with teeth
to minimise the harm they can do.
Remember: people take note of the nails.
We recommend the following uses
for your hands: point, applaud, shake,
scratch, catch, throw, write, stroke,
clutch, clench, chop, cut, slap (hard).
If you dare, let them roam on a piano,
if you don't, teach them how to press buttons.*
Gingerly, she puts them on. They fit like gloves.

John Foulcher

Where the March Hare runs

Political leaders preen themselves and their dangerous nonsense might be someone's absurd tea party—except the ludicrousness is real. In our dreams we find greater senselessness everywhere, making weird landscapes and unfamiliar houses. People are acting like they've never done in life and their behaviour's luridly compelling. Where the March Hare runs we follow and so many commonsense assumptions are subject to the Red Queen's logic. Every night the news endorses curious improbabilities ...

Paul Hetherington

After Martin Carter,
'This is the Dark Time, My Love'

this is the dreich time, my love.
with you seems possible a knife
avoids windmill anatomy of rivers
called of blood in & of these islands,
called by rebroadcast fascists
in constant rehistorying.
this is the dreich time, my love,
marslight max failyours feelyours,
swich balance of sound gents ration-
all, witch maaks all lunacy mine,
kalibrates blackwhite my rubi
shoes vnder the windup moonlight
vntill my field of possibylities
pines to a label. yet knot with you

Vahni Capildeo

Gone fishing

He called me in a coke-crazed haze from Albuquerque.
He'd gone fishing. The line was pretty bad
and there was soccer on TV—it was hard to follow
the drift... but when Costacurta forced a corner

*

the sound of Mr Wang's legendary rooftop karaoke
echoed across the moonlit pond where Jack Horner,
fellow writer, had already fallen in, his blonde head
bobbing among the floats, surely a martini too many

*

for a midnight hunt of what looked like a quirky
cross between artichoke and armadillo. No, we said.
We'd rather have a go at '(The Way to) Amarillo',
possibly something by the Quo, or maybe

*

he was mistaking me for Paolo Maldini, the jerky,
half-time text onscreen—in auto-translation
from Chinese—the commentary to our oblivion
as we executed, thumbs in belts, a near perfect grebo.

Paul Munden

Some assembly required

You feel you are being followed   Perhaps it is only the wires
out the window of the train   They are tracing your suspended

journey in liquorice parallels travelling and travelling hovering
in an infinite deferral   of touch   Perhaps you are pretending

it is Sunday, sprawling over a seat and a seat and a seat   all lax,
all lone and fluid   Perhaps you resent the man who shuffles on

at Milson's Point   who lowers and sighs to sit   right thigh
jammed against yours   At the same time perhaps you realise

this was always going to happen   it has only been a matter of time
You may struggle to accept the gift of his odour,   his aura

of urine and cigarette   his breath like lighter fluid   You note he is
wearing work clothes   and some kind of lanyard   You may be tremored,

slightly,   by the jiggling of his right thigh   He is Morse-coding
someone   steadily, intently   jiggling and jiggling   He sings himself,

softly, *helme helme melme flo flo helme gelme*   You are intent
on the window   on the wires   on the never-ending oblong of their

refusal to meet   *helme helme melme flo flo helme gelme ouw*
Perhaps   if you looked at him now   you would see flames

pour from his mouth, feel the shock of his words carbonising
between his teeth   *helme helme helpme getme ouu*   Beyond the wires

you are watching a structure approach   somewhere near Artarmon
with every jiggle   the pieces assemble themselves   into a beacon

some kind of communications   tower   *helme helpme getme flo*
flo helme gelme out   The thing is an elegant   bricolage   a model

with the joins inked in   Perhaps you did not notice the baby
get on at Wollstonecraft   but it is incontrovertibly here, now

redly refusing to breastfeed   wailing   *Helme helpme melme flo*
flo helme getme ouuu   You are still watching the structure approach

the baby is an elegant   bricolage   its cries are carbonising   somewhere
between Milson's Point and Artarmon   it would eat   the liquorice

parallels   if it could   it wants the wires   to cross   Perhaps you look down
to realise   you also are wearing work clothes   and some kind of lanyard

and by now   you fully comprehend   the structure   You sing yourself,
softly *helme helpme gelme flo flo helme getme out*   Perhaps you realise

it is time   it has always been time   for you   to get to work

Melinda Smith

No reason

beyond art

Turning another page, staying up late
And unsupervised so far

Into maturity. Like all women,

I'm told, I aspire to a certain stability
And may have believed it would be

Supplied by heavy ballast, say

Marble, though we've all been given
The pedestal warning and taken heed.

Taken head, I might rather say, and strong.

Maybe an anchor would be better. Forgetting
An anchor hooks by chain to something

Equally heavy. A battleship. A heart.

Katharine Coles

When myth turns to truth

Losing our common memories, we rehearse each other's lines. To be honest, he said, I'm not that keen on language. I kissed him, hard, tongue in throat. How about now? I asked as he stumbled back. He turns into tree, he turns into bird flying through the tops of trees, singing in sudden harmony with his new family. Myth is the only true story. And me? I am dog. Still hoping to have my day.

Jen Webb

Knuckle down

Field log: the mythology of crust says unyielding, over-baked railings contain magical properties not found elsewhere. Crust holds particular magical sway over hair, said to grow or thicken chest hirsuteness and/or generate curl—neither of which are desired despite the consumption of crust as being desired by traditional elders. Crust is a threshold food signalling the material barrier between pleasure and satiation. Discussed in light of bone grinding to prove dough, and as such, the crust mythos upholds Frazer's original speculations of fertility worship.

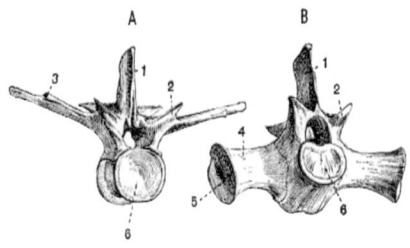

Monica Carroll

Saru, the monkey god, describes a laundromat in Kyoto

Saru was able
to describe the moon,
What would he make
of this small room?
A room of moons? A need for change?
The folding away of smalls?

An old woman does sudoku.
The bodhisattva emerges,
splits her face in two.

Shane Strange

In your language

for Mel (Amanda) Baggs

weeeeee aaaaarrrrreeee
wheeeeerrrrrrrreeeeeee
weeeeeeee aaarrrrreeee
weeeee hhhheeeeaarrrr
aaaaaiiiiiiirrrrrrrrrrrrrr
weeerrreeeee aaawwwe
weeeee eeeeaaaaarrrrrr
weeee aarrrre herrrrrre

scra scru sski scra sckri
scra scru ssck sscra scri
scru ssck scru sck scraa
shuuup tck shhhupp tck
shhhhhuuup tck tck tck
shhp prrressss prrressss
prresss prrressss prresss

rrrrraaaccckkkeeetttttt
rrraacckkkeeettt racket
butitsstruckbutitsstruck
butitsstruckbutitsstruck

weeee aarrrre herrrrrre
weeee aarrrre aaaiiiirrr

you're standing at the window, back
to camera, as the droning song of things
flows through you and out of your mouth
your arms, rhythmic, insistent, without translation
and these tree limbs—bare as my ignorance—
shiver just slightly, in response

what qualifies as language or as being here?
to brush, shake, stroke or rub unlocks
the speech of objects, your every
surface and cavity resonates—pushing
your face into an open book, you sense
the meaning of paper is not just in the ink

you sniff, caress and take into your mouth
each tactile form, yet they say you're imprisoned
in yourself—what does it matter
if some think you're too rehearsed or capable
for the diagnosis, or if all this is a performance,
sound poetry as a way of living, when

there are these wordless speaking things?
touched, they ring like instruments and enter us
heeeerrrree whheerree wee are

Andy Jackson

S P A C E

Space

Mostly what we're made of, our solid concepts keep meeting it. Pressed into smallness, my father lay in a vast amount—the man who'd stood tall in my life and dressed me with presence. He said little, although he'd been more eloquent than any of us, as if another mouth sucked his words; as if already outside his life while an inarticulate actor stood in. I embraced his familiar body but the man himself was abstract. We shuffled; I thought of open oceans and deserts; skying acres of thin and blown air. Down-to-earth, he said, 'I've decided to die'. Space shifted and jostled.

Paul Hetherington

Erasure after William Empson's 'Aubade' (1)

standing

deaths
      bawl

      blank
you   have seen   a
      heart

Vahni Capildeo

The silent builders

The silent builders are raising
a house on the bare block beside us.
Each day I watch them loading
brick onto brick, lifting steel beams
or standing about with nail guns
and drills. But they make no sound,

say nothing. One of them
leans to a radio, tunes it to music
no one can hear. Then his fingers
clamp on a hammer, swing it
to the mute wood, the trembling frame
of the house becoming a house.

In the stiffening slurry of quiet,
foundations for a ground floor
are boxed in with a slab of cement,
then more walls, a first storey,
ribbons of knotted wood sealing
the rooms in their emptiness.

Soon the silent builders will pack
and go, the rooms will sprout
frail tendrils of noise. In the end
the house will bloom with
music, footsteps, children's cries,
laughter, screaming, sobbing, silence.

John Foulcher

red, white and window

The April air above the office blocks is guileless blue
but too warm to trust. On the corner there is a situation, cordoned off,
   a jumble

of witches' hats and high-vis. The building says *nab*. The logo
   is a bloodied red star. One point
is striped with absences, sharp parallel scars, twin zebra-marks
   of gouge, they gesture

to the window washer, white helmeted, in his slowly rising cage, who
   tends to the dust. He bathes
the glass which is keeping the air out, the workers in. He thinks *nab*
   means opportune theft.
Inside, on the window ledge, a dusty white peace lily calls
   to the white helmet. Beside it a woman

with a headset and bitten nails, her roots starting to show. Her screen
   says *nab*. She tends to it
like a duty, like dusty window, it does not always obey, there are
   wilful red absences

starting to show. In her mind, a dream of a day with no gouges, no
   glass, a portal she sails through,
opportunely, on a Vespa, in a sundress, past all the situations,
   unmarked again, impossible to catch.

Melinda Smith

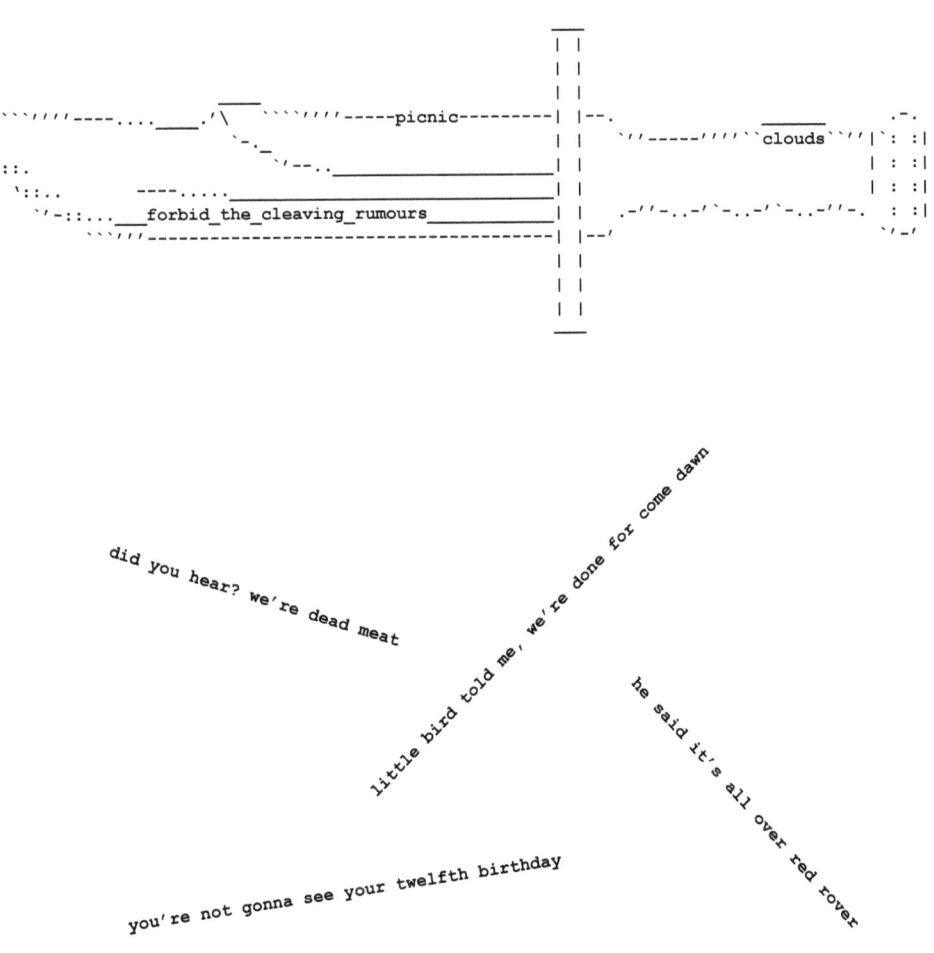

Monica Carroll

Beyond the walls

You open the door and watch as cats spill out of the house and across the lawn. Behind you, the muted song of whitegoods; ahead there's only space. You have laundry to hang out, a wheelie-bin to take down the drive, bills to pay. Always bills to pay. This isn't how you had imagined the future. If you had made better choices. If you had made any choices. Now here you are, you and the cats and four small rooms and a roof that needs attention, but gradually the space ahead of you resolves into landscape, and above you a hot air balloon hisses as it scoops up a handful of sky, and you start to think about setting sail.

Jen Webb

Flight

In the space between
hairline and left eyebrow
Yuri Gagarin—Galactic Hero—
had a scar the shape
of a kerbstone's kiss
where he fell face first
after tripping from a balcony
while trying to escape
Valentina Goryacheva
who found him in bed
with a nurse called Anna.

Shane Strange

Instructions for client restraint

to minimise disruption for others and in order for us to get anything done around here sometimes it has to be cobbled together with wooden planks and chicken wire you can't call it a cage it's more a withdrawal space with padlocks on the outside and a warning this report contains unreliable testimony difficult behaviours screaming complex needs no other options codes of practice expert care these burdens are tragic this construction a space where he might quieten down or scream into exhaustion or maybe try extra medication adrenal fatigue low pay high turnover lack of training thrown in the deep no doubt it can be distressing for family members to hear about every single incident a report is made and fled again it won't be accessible disability always is other people the oversight challenged is shrugged off as the funding evaporates there is no-one there as if creates a strange peacefulness at the centre a pacified body is a space of restraint against the person who cleans you clothes you is there while you sleep vulnerable non-verbal or immobile people either way how to make a complaint who would believe her anyway the work may attract a few bad apples access to own good strapped into a chair or bed or toilet seat unable to consent or speak bruises can't say what happened restraint marks on the wrists and ankles for their

Andy Jackson

Floor plan

Off the foyer, the guestroom.
The kitchen with its oven

Ticking, the living room
Where I won't invite you. Pipes

Chur, and the bedroom
Fills with shadows and tum-

bled sheets. Down the hall
One does her thinking, keeping

The door shut. And what
Dim passage directs

Your yon and hither,
Your in, your out?

Katharine Coles

'Road closed'

was emphatic,
but the rusty sign
hung on an open gate,
allowing him to kid himself
and drive on through—
up the narrow sandy track
in an erratic

       sequence
       of hairpin bends
       towards the summit,
       and as he continued,
       with ever less option
       to reverse, he began to forget
       the warning, his lapsed

judgement eclipsed
by glimpses of magnificence
beyond—hills, folding
to a pale blue
infinity—
until the sudden, huge stone
fallen into the road.

       He felt the absurdity
       as he tried first to move it,
       then—back in the car, holding
       his nerve—to gauge the space
       between rock
       and scarp,
       all to within an inch

of his life.
And for what?—
the view from the top?
His sense of privilege
was equally a trespass
on the sublime.
He longed to remain

        in the melancholy
        of his private wilderness
        with time
        and empty sky his friends,
        rather than once again
        face the crumbling precipice
        of his own folly.

Paul Munden

PLEASURE

Apes rule

Use pearl—
pale, sure
   pearl. Use
purse. Ale.

Leer up as
re-use pal;
re-use lap.

Pure sale.

*Pa, reel us,
repeal us,
repel us*: a
user plea.

A repulse.

Pale ruse,
pleasure.

Lures ape;
rules ape.

Melinda Smith

He marvels

at how her glistening pink nails,
pressed into the bed,
seem to keep her suspended
as her body ripples
with oceanic swell
and her nipples
like bright coral
quiver towards the light,

but how too—after a lull—
he can feel
her flex again and vanish
fish-
like into the night.

Paul Munden

Organ recital

The mind likes to think the mind
Chats with itself, amusing

Outside-in. In this
It resembles the heart, no more

In order, I hate to say, no less
Reflexive. It's the way a man's organ

Has been said to lead him around
By the nose, as it were. Said by men,

Mind, not me. If you believe reports,
Like him all I can do is follow.

Katharine Coles

There are many pleasures

        the first has your mouth flush with milk taste of clear
blue sky sounds of soft fur sweet smell of sun and shadow
        in a blur of senses gently vexing everything rushing in
was that how it was back then before you could hold
            words or make memory these pleasures (making you)

        others you soon realise are built from detritus and thin air
your first bike and a vacant lot of roller-coaster dirt paths
        pocket-money shrapnel swapped for a bag of mixed sugars
blue bruises twisted ankles accidental scars compelling
            as they're absorbed slowly into the flesh (alchemical)

        but what version of it makes you the only one not laughing
your marrow registering that acid attention before you do
        a joke a shove a name to become punchline and exile but
pinned there and kept as someone else's strange pleasure
            the little needles of that sound still inside you (as ballast)

        this one is timid and hides when you take out your pen
but unwatched it'll sneak into the ink or disguise itself
        as the seeds of tears or kisses the soft percussion of rain
your breath fizzing feather-soft through mirror-neurons
            as thought grows tired and unclenches (a hinge creaks)

        then there's her wise palm tender on your cheek
that crack in your frost would be pleasure enough
        but to see something pure welling up from the centre
of her chest to know she has surfaced through fathomless
            pain into herself this frail and fierce light (

Andy Jackson

So far, she's missing

from the set
I fascinate & live off.
   My travels foam
with heely girls:
I can haz wet whenever.
   What I want from her
is More & Other.
I'll enter by the Kingsway.
   Earworm her,
trek into her wriggling
braindom, hardman her boneless dream.
   Total invasion
by tiny interference.
O my Criseyde, my chrysalid!
   Her cryptic's missing
in my mouth: my tongue
sprouts teeth, turns against this poor soft
   palate. I must
complete the set
I fascinate & live off.
   There are few synonyms
for the creature
I anticipate. No? No?
   I will loose.

Vahni Capildeo

Surfing the waves

Merman, presenting his tongue. Doesn't matter whether he comes bearing paroxysms of delight or emptying your purse, he is always the one you wanted, the one you get, he will do the right thing, will find the beat, he will hit that sweet spot: he is the rip in the tide, the sun's shudder as it slips over the horizon and splashes into the further line of sea; he is that weekend you took all those years ago that you regretted so much the next day but later not, but later absolutely not.

Jen Webb

This is what it feels like

We're in the boat, on the bed, rolling down the grassy bank. I am pulled along through darkness to a patch of light. And we play. My fingers rub catching up the noiseless squeaks as I strum across the taut inside skins of you. The perfection of the world passes into. It hurts, as an ache, it hurts.

Monica Carroll

Through eye-gate, and ear-gate into the city of child-soul

At first
> it may not be very pleasant
> for a boy to go to school.

He prefers
> not to exert himself;
> not to put forth any mental effort.

But as it becomes
> more and more natural to him,
> he comes to love study.

At first,
> the doing of the right
> affords us but very little pleasure,

yet
> we are to continue to do right.

And
> after a while it becomes pleasant for us to do right.

Gradually,
> year after year,
> the river wears its course
> deeper and deeper,

until finally
> through the soft soil and the hard rock
> the boy is broken.

Shane Strange

Gathering

In the middle of morning, after lying through six months of his own empty unrest, he gathered his body as if in a bag and drove to the coast. The ocean welcomed his thrashing strokes; thin-stretched glimmers caressed his goose-bumped skin. He rode the rip until he was a long way out, feeling the swell of thought subside, feeling the pleasure of being carried into deeper rhythms. When the surfer found him, hauling him back to clear air, molluscs climbed from his skin; crawling words dived away; claims of gravity and his heart's pulse asserted themselves. He dressed again in the idea of himself though it fitted so much more loosely, climbing back towards his profession. He paused, then, to remember.

Paul Hetherington

On pleasure

At Riveaulx Abbey,
we puzzle about the purpose
of these ruined rooms.
Nothing excludes.
I stand inside the portal,
feel a breeze no one would have known
in the time of distinctions.
Like nuns processing,
daisies offer their small chalices
to the bees, who whisper their insect sins.

John Foulcher

IDENTITY

On a carefree afternoon such as this

I might wander down the steep gravel drive and follow the long slow bend of the road where banks of rhododendrons make a pink and purple blind spot ... on past the woods to tap my stick on the village hall door: I'm welcomed in by those clearing the tea, ladies who see through me and the ill-matched colour of my beard, my grease-painted wrinkles—I can still smell the spirit gum, feel the itch of stretched skin as I tried to speak in a low voice and fake an old man's gait, but I can't catch my mother's eye, can't gauge how half a century has no doubt changed her face as it has mine, or how we might yet disentangle ourselves from the scene...

Paul Munden

Thought experiment

Imagine there is a skin—a permeable textile of some kind—a raw silk, or damask linen. For this poem, imagine the textile—X—stretched in a hoop frame. It strains tight. Can be thrum-beaten as a mild drum. In my palm sleeps a knife. Delicate copper pins penetrate the antler handle. What happens when quenched martensitic steel, and pure-dyed mulberry silk, meet? We have ways we tell this out: the knife cuts the silk, the silk has a gash. What was not possible is now possible. I can slide two fingers in, through. I can hear us inside. She feels my knuckles. We make another land.

Monica Carroll

Bloodnut gut-wrench

In the front window of Salty Joe's, a red-haired
man is sipping tomato juice, scanning the horizon, eyes
on the scarred grey sea   Snarling into his phone
I told you, I have a couple of days
at the most   I avoid his ice eyes, shuddering
at his orangutan head, at the hair on his
forearms, a matted almost-pelt of fishing wire, gone
burred and sandy   They are mutants, you know   All
the red-haired blue-eyed people descend from the same gamechanger,
the same alien   A man can be a man
and yet apart, an animal, mottled, exotic, a giraffe
sitting in the front window of Salty Joe's, wearing
the face of the Vikings, the Normans   His snarl
is the sound of a sweaty melee, beaching, leaping
a keel   Only melanomas can kill them   No home
but the restless salty sea   I know in my
bones they are bad   (am relieved my own auburn
has silvered to frost, my own freckles have paled
on my hull   that the fire-haired changeling I carried
is silent   is drowned) and I know in my
bones   that the raiding is starting again   He sips
juice   The corners of his mouth run with dark
tomato   *Yeah let's get on it*   told you   Bloody
boat people   inexorable   our axes will sing again   soon

Melinda Smith

Epistemology

At the hospital, you hovered over
Mum's last breaths, which, the way
you told it, seemed as if she were hauling
a heavy weight up a steepening incline.
I sprawled across her abandoned bed,
minding your daughters and watching TV,
a test between Australia and Pakistan.
When the phone rang at last, it erupted
like a bowler appealing for the faintest edge.
Can you bring the girls now? you asked
between breaths. *Should I tell them?*
You held your breath, then handed me
the moment. The older girl belched out tears.
The younger, who was so close to Mum,
turned to stone and went to freshen up
before we left. Decades later, I ask
myself if it had happened that way,
or did I contrive it, a comfort in knowing.
The scent of my mother's skin, on those sheets.

John Foulcher

Beauty, from the other side

Aged twelve, before surgery to fix the scoliosis, I formed
an idea a certain girl might like me. I found her beautiful.
Or was it just that I knew others did? I can't be sure.
I don't think we ever spoke. What I do remember
are the insults I absorbed like splinters, how my body
held and resisted them. Like nested dolls, each identity

contains within itself another, contrary identity.
Who am I, apart from what others assume? A deformed
person appears banished from sex by their own body,
into the solitude of knowing that being beautiful
can be studied like a distant, dying star. Remember
those soft-porn images of lace and curves? I was sure

such skin would touch this skin, but never sure
exactly how. That was a time unaware of identity—
awash in the thrill and vertigo, I became a member
of that boy's club I couldn't belong to (I was deformed).
I held in my flesh a pre-used sense of what beautiful
meant, some detached assessment of another body.

What else to do but accept, like death, this body?
So far from desirable, I might surface on the other shore
where the soft fall of light on skin is what's beautiful—
a way of seeing, not what's seen. A stigmatised identity
can fuel anyone's resentment. Why say *deformed*
or *crippled*, when there's *striking* or even *sexy*? Remember

who keeps slamming doors in your face, remember
the nauseating, clinical chill of those rooms—each body
shaved, veiled with cosmetics, or cut and deformed
by surgeons, for *beauty*. Can anyone be sure
breaking their way in will change anything? An identity
like this might make me a fetish, but not *beautiful*.

I've only heard it spoken in whispers—*beautiful*—
by other exiles. Such tenderness is harder to remember
than cruelty, feels more frail than any given identity.
Both words and electricity surge through the body—
concepts and their fractures—so even you're unsure
what might spill out. That's why this poem is formed

around words like *beautiful*—they're more deformed
than any of us, whatever we remember. All that's sure
is they lose their identity in the depths of every body.

Andy Jackson

Methods for the identification of individuals, living or dead

Contacting you through this letter is not with the intention of distracting you with my *Intents and Purposeful Endeavour*. I have found you in a *Quest For A Last Name* like that of a late customer—Mister Ferago Strange—a *Business Tycoon* who lived in Hong Kong for nine years. He passed on with his immediate family in a *Ghastly Motor Accident*, without appointing a *Next Of Kin* for his estate. Before the abovementioned *Ugly Catastrophe*, a lump sum of $35,700,000 was placed with us for safe keeping. My suggestion to you is that, I would like to present you as the *Next Of Kin And Beneficiary* to this deposit to *Prevent Confiscation of the Unclaimed Funds* by the treasury of the bank of china. The law that allows this confiscation is *Unjust And Inhuman* as it often creates avenues for the top officials to divert such fortunes for their *Own Selfish Use*. I will now put your name as *Next Of Kin* and I will prepare the *Legal Documentation* that will assist to facilitate the release of the fund to you without any *Breach Of The Law*. Note that I have worked out all modalities to complete the transaction successfully.

Be Rest Assured That The Transaction Is 100% Legal And Risk Free.

Shane Strange

The man in the street

The man in the street is not me, though he tilts his head in the same way. The boy I remember isn't me, though he stares from the past's frame with a recognisable insouciance. The identity I dressed in isn't me—I was naïve, believing in words as if they were pure. The weight they carried hadn't occurred to me; their reckless way of doing what they will. I thought my mouthings were my own. Perhaps all we have is happenstance, and wary stabs at being; waking at night to wonder. The decisions that made us crowd and talk.

Paul Hetherington

Scaling the walls

Summer time, and jacaranda blossoms drift along the ICB, and I do too, driving past Kay Gee while you say I'd rather be in Venice. Not in this city of hard ground and liquid sky, of fly-away streets, roads that burrow underground all knot and weave. We are going nowhere. It is 3,400 kilometres to Darwin and *let's go,* you said, grabbing me, *let's light out and head north.* Yes. Yes. Just past the Wivenhoe I lost heart; I turned back. Each morning now I cut carrots into strips, pick the fragments of shell off my boiled egg. I put my lunchbox in my bag and lock the door and wait for a bus, any bus. Somewhere else another me, all misplaced faith, is with you in our small blue car, lighting out, heading north.

Jen Webb

Dog tag

Smaller than my dog
And differently proportioned

I stalked the west side.
My coat, like his, was black.

Back then, if you wanted
To pacify a man

You had to let him touch you.
Some parts stay the same. Mostly

I declined, thinking
That's what power smells like,

Who needs it? The dog agreed.
In truth, he outweighed me

By a good fifty percent.
Passersby mistook him,

Jumping at their own shadows.
His wagging helped nothing.

Of course, I sympathised,
But what else could I tell him?

Full of hands, the world
Offered a body to touch, but

People lowered their eyes
And sidled slowly by.

Katharine Coles

Hear her relax release

grammar case by case
like dressage like a dressing
like a dismount like a mountain
like a tourniquet like a ticket
tossed into, sunlit-perfect,
the high throat of a non-combustible bin.
Hem him wired withered
like a horse's tail like silver tinsel
like a salon floor like ashes
like a sequence like a challenge
in the grassy selving syntax
of a Roman road, direct, no
longer taken. Ai my
love, this is none of us.
A plague of visitors upon this place.
A ring of lucifers upon this flyer.
A famine of genders upon these permissions.
A mean of colours upon this slip.

Vahni Capildeo

RHYTHM

If there were five people

1.
If there were five people. Two will remember. Two will forget. One will recall as picnic.

1.
We own the sea for one week. Furious with threads. You joke about violence. Stab. Stab. Stab.

2.
The scraps fray.

3.
Felt is an is and a do. Before loom, spindle, needle, was felt. Smash one thing into another, a squirt of damp, two become lost. Break and fuse. By no means a forge. We don't cheat with fire in felt.

5.
We turned over 41 shells. Then 6 more. The waves. Break. The waves. Break. Break shell. Felted sand is stone.

8.
We lay tufts, hanks, between the plates of our picnic. Trouble the threads with blows to mend grotesque memory tatters.

13.
Almost convinced by the monster's urge, Frankenstein pieced scraps to craft the monster a companion. He smashed and stabbed but ceased.

21.
We shake out the cracker crumbs. Daring the seagulls to swoop ever near.

Monica Carroll

Lines from an ECG

for Norman Jackson (1926—1973)

the heart is not a precision instrument—
                listen, now, it seems to stop and
start and stop and start, as if ambivalent—
                no metronome but a poem of muscle

with an iambic limping—I am, I am
                almost the age you were when yours
failed and you fell from a hospital bed
                into the unsaid—*diastole* and *systole*,

how these chambers fill with blood and
                love, then urgently send them back out—
the heart's door, always swinging on
                its hinges—surely the aorta must tire

of this back and forth, contract, relax, old
                unsolvable argument of flesh—between
each beat, a tiny pause, spark that will
                one day expand to fill the whole

body—the problem, not any imperfection
                in its rhythm, but how too much pressure
can open a tear in the wall—yes, I must
                get checked, each year, each year—

now as the ECG turns my insistent metre
                into sound, I hear whale song sped-up,
then the slow-motion crack of a whip—
                the cold silence underneath—

Andy Jackson

Once more with feeling

River not a flow
but a slow adjustment
of liquid. Where the rocks
and sands dive below
our feet dive deep be-
neath our feet and we are
left afloat in tannin
stained water we tell ourselves

if you think of the below,
of the rocks and mud
and the unknown deep.
If you think of the below,
of the unknown deep
cold in your stomach—
in the small circumference
of your heart.

If you think of the below,
of the unknown deep,
I will not save you,
I will let you drown.

Shane Strange

A summer in the tundra

After every freeze they lay her out, ankle to ankle, hands across her breasts. Routinely they tend her: food and washing and waste. Staff bend low, so close she can count the pores on their skin, breathe their toothpaste and their tea. Her heart is beating, her feet tapping the rhythm of blood, the rhythm of ceiling tiles; her heart is listening to the faint music of footfall and trolleys and phones. Eventually they haul her back, the blood returns to her flesh, they send her on her way. Outside is the sky. Outside is the conurbation and the promise that if she lives clean, for just a little longer, the ice will welcome her home.

Jen Webb

Accidental

What I shouldn't throw over
The handlebars. Caution,

Wind: nothing broken
This time but rhythm gone rough

And tumble, soft tissue
Fileting, tomorrow ripening

Plums to ice. Already
Thinking all this before

It happens, then my head
Enters time. Crack.
                  Writing

A poem, my Buddhist friend
Will say, write a poem. And

A bicycle—or is it
The other way? What is

One to make of the old one-
Two, my heart's

Kachunk fully occupied
In song? In retrospect,

I pivot into the downhill
Spinning hard and seeing

No gravel or pothole, only
Words bumping

And grinding, in and out
By turn, in return undone.

                                    Katharine Coles

Beating the mix

I remember my mother beating
a rhythm in the cake mix, the *whack!*
of the spoon against the sides of the bowl,
the blend of the days with only her
and me and the whirl of butter and sugar.
We'd sit together on the back step,
the yard cartoon-green in the morning
light, the fibro walls of the house
the luminous white of television.
I hovered over the bowl, the solo
of the spoon. I didn't want the taste
to be soured by flour, but when
the churning was over, the music done,
she took it to the oven, where the mix
was transformed and diminished,
which happens to most things we make.

John Foulcher

After Sir Philip Sidney, Astrophil and Stella 31

Wth hw sd stps (i, uh, aaah)
      O MOON . . .
Hw slntl… hw wn… !
Wht   tht
tht   rch sh rp rrws
        O   O
  O   O O
      OO
   ee

O MOON

constantlovewantofwitconstantlovewant
ofwitconstantlovewantofwitconstant

    rubies   red   you   mine be   here
are beauties proud? are beauties proud? here. be.

  are   you above love? the fisherman waits
above love be lov'd and yet

   stiltwalkers exact vengeance firemen dance on ladders
o lovers scorn o love o possess

ohhh ah uh you air uh
              ffff
            FULLlllness

Vahni Capildeo

Jazz quartet

Wander in, take a wine
       at the little table, red
in the chipped glass, old red
like the lip-stain at the rim, ghost-red
reflected in the sugarbowl, see it spread
like the velvet curtains at the back, got your head
in a fine place, the same place
       where the bass is walking at a walking pace,
under all the ladders, on a roll,
a fat swagger, talking to a talking face
with a soul in a mad blabber, stalking to a spun wheel,
a stagger for the genteel
a plucked line, a strung puppet but it's not mine,
a long spine, a flip to a winning hum
       a drum whisper, a stutter quick
tick of the tipsy clock, a slick
snare skipping softly to an under-slip
carrying a big stick
a brush hushing to a finger click,
sleight of hands in a summer trick
       piano in a hurry, coming down
scurry bumble on the slung stairs, the old brown
the dirty rum, pass the muddled jugs round
to the huddled scrum, hit the floor
the sure switch, the doors twitch, start the running
with the rising cup, coming up, stalk and spin
with the crystal napkin rings, swing a grin as you slither in
to the idea   of a chandelier   the brittle glitter,
       the sweet shine, the sax pouring honey wet
down the bannisters, the swoop and spread,
the wide howl and the dog's dead, the big bed
with the feathers and the foghorns, where you let

loose balloons in the wide sky, let
the white tiger out, and he stops by,
        mute as the new sun
coming up, the shop's shut
game's up, done and dusted like the long night
the lost fight, the wrong light shining in your strong wine
pleads you to leave it for a long time

'til tomorrow will be just fine
        'til tomorrow will be just fine

Melinda Smith

With daily practice

his stiff fingers found
a music of their own,
the muscle memory of his arm
a rhythm akin
to the unique routine

of a bird of paradise,
waiting for her to come
to his patch of ground
and allow him to impress.

Paul Munden

Syncopation

A hawk makes the unknowable sky in wingbeats and blood-thresh; a train marks a metronome way through suburbs. There's a fallback and run-forward of waves—a skiff shifting, turning, becoming more movement than object; and on the sand a man genuflects, his thought a syncopation as sun and wind collide. The rhythm is what he hears, it momentarily quietens his sense of being. It's not a heartbeat, or the world shuddering in its pyroclastic turbulence, but the gesture and movement of every unstill thing.

Paul Hetherington

ACCURACY

A very small history of reading

If the modest adjustment to perception
afforded by the microscope
revealed to Robert Hooke the precision
'of *point* commonly so call'd
that is the mark of a *full stop*, or *period*'
as '*smutty daubings* …
a great splatch of *London* dirt'

what are we to make of Meric Casaubon
who prescribed courses of histories
to those suffering 'heighten'd passions'
and recounted the case of two monarchs
cured beyond medical science
by reading Quintus Curtius
and Livy's *History of Rome?*

Shane Strange

What do you mean by 'fake'?

                                              By 'news'?
If the sky is falling, do you hunt meteors

Or raise your umbrella? Keep your head
Down, take cover, my word but this

Gets worse and worse. In your nit-
Picky life, what did you ever

Want from mountains, endless
Autumn flaming, this blue, blue sky?

Katharine Coles

Marks

(or, Lt Wm Bligh notes the distinguishing features of the Bounty mutineers)

It is given to so few of us,
this clarity

Fletcher Christian Aged 24 years 5'9' High	
Complexion	Dark, & very swarthy
Hair	Blackish or very dark brown
Make	Strong
Marks	Star tattooed on the left breast and on the backside. His knees stands a little out and may be called a little bow-legged

(They have left him his pen
He is making a kind of ledger,
scratching at the bitter pages

as if these columns
will ever balance)

George Stewart Aged 23 years 5'7' High	
has the	small face and black eyes

of all your bad luck
scurrying straight at you, a rat
across a mooring-rope

(He will make proper account, for there will be a reckoning
Adrift though he is, he will tally the blackguards
like stolen cargo, like the lost breadfruit seedlings
—months and months of His Majesty's work
thrown into the sea)

Peter Haywood Aged 17, 5' 7'	
and	well-proportioned
	had not done growing

—as if such a wound, such a theft, is ever done growing—

his	Manx accent

will convict him, apparently—that and

his	three-legged tattoo

The Pacific has blotted the ink, we will never know whether

Edward Young Aged 22, stood 5'1' or 5'7'	
but he remains	Dark of complexion,
	Strong of make,
has	Rather a bad look,
has	lost several of his foreteeth and those that remain are all rotten

This clarity
given to so few
This certainty

that what we have lost
was lost on this day
at this hour
at the hands of a man

with	*a small mole*
	on the left side of the throat

Did the Chiefs of O-Taheite
keep their own
ledger of thieves
dealers in bad faith
liars

Did they note somewhere
each particular indignity
so many women kidnapped
so many houses burned, so many canoes
so many balances of power
left holed, left listing

The grandmothers must have
surely
inside their implacable heads

—the litany of wounds, of thefts, is never done growing

They have always known
when someone commandeers
your only vessel
sails it clean away

the recital
of each imperfection
may be all the lifeboat

that is left to you

how it can then become
a matter of utmost importance
that the perpetrator

	is	*subject to violent perspiration and particularly in his hands so that he soils any thing he handles*

Melinda Smith

Clockwork

Every now and then,
when the slowing
rotation of the earth
puts the caesium
atoms out of joint,
it's your given task

to over-write time.
You know the risk—
how in the moment
of adjustment
things can go awry:
a reliquary may be

spirited back home
or a financial killing
get away scot free.
You walk across
the open plan office
that's cased in glass

like a skeleton clock,
your fingers turning
a small brass wheel,
the rack and pinion
that raises the spring
to quicken the dead-

beat lock and glide.
Bi-metallic strips
of the pendulum
gauge the day's heat
and compensate
almost to perfection,

the seemingly lazy
swing giving impulse
to the running seconds
and those subsidiaries:
minutes and hours.
The escapement

is all—the very same
shift as the carriage
of clean white space
into this beating path
of alphabetical lead,
a precise location

for your thoughts—
following the dark
snicket into the yard
where the toyshop
of your childhood
should be, if only

the restoring force
held good. How you
long to repair each
worn brass cog,
ache to recalibrate
every harmonic

oscillation of loss,
to somehow bring
the bewildering drag
of years to account;
tethering an angel
to follow the sun.

Paul Munden

Quiver

They cluster in the mouth
like arrows in a quiver—
pithy, shaped summations;
honed phrases struck from
language, straightened and
smoothed. The strung bow is
lifted and one by one they're
discharged—querulous,
incisive, sharp-tongued. But
words aren't as efficient; their
tips are blunt even after filing;
their heft is less certain than
wood, flint or bronze. And the
word 'arrow' is often clumsy
in the mouth, unable to be set
free. Still: 'he let fly, and his
arrow pierced every one of the
handle-holes of the axes from
the first onwards till it had
gone right through them.'

Paul Hetherington

By the river of

He took two things and stole one. A knife with a sabre clip blade, a blue tarpaulin and six sausages suffocating under their plastic-tight covers. The tarp we slept under as night swallowed us down. Sausages met fire. The knife twitched with hunger.

Monica Carroll

An atheist for God

My eyes are not the same eyes. I see
through frosted glass, only long memories
have an edge. Years ago, after my son
turned twenty, I took him to an optometrist—
he had always thought the world
vague, and we were always distracted.
When he slipped on his first pair
of spectacles, the world's spectacle slipped
from a fog, on the road to Damascus.
I remember the way he stared
at his hands, the delicate leaves, distance.
I remember a parent's guilt.
                        This morning,
wandering glassless in the library,
I glimpse a book, high up. *An Atheist
for God*. Taking it down, I see
I've been wrong, again. I hold the book,
A Thirst for God, lightly in my hand.

John Foulcher

Erasure after William Empson's 'Aubade' (2)

Hours
                              could take

          up

    large
             buildings

The guarded

                                rest
       the best thing

The language
                    for lying

Vahni Capildeo

No relief maps

after 'Silent Treatment' (digital print), by Cameron May

what do I know about weather | these storms | that
pummel and erode | only we're all brought closer |
to collapse | already inching through | our own
unhomely terrains | daydream | flesh | so close
our tremors | overlap | walls crack | where do I
end and you begin | we are each in the body |
of the other | but think ourselves alone | or are
wrenched there by pain | sometimes I'm afraid
I've lost you | that you may have lost your self
| what good are these hands | against the un
known | surgeons offer | cold white theatre
lights | divide us into | exact fragments for
ease of access | specialists make us motion
less and quiet | who knew | our insides |
could be so much like landscapes | no relief
maps | oceanic | just an idea of order in the
background | we're spilling over | and out |
one symptom | crashes into another | wait
ing room and examination | everything un
settled | tests come back | inconclusive |
my love | adrift | speechless | this tidal
rip | where's that one useful word | who
can say | what's ruined | what survives
| even a diagnosis only | comes from
outside | how to cope here | now?

Andy Jackson

The cartographer

It's called a mappa mundi, the teacher said. Use the right terms, idiot boy. Idiot boy turned the page of his foxed notebook and began to draw. Christ-on-a-cross hovering in a capital T over the soup plate of the world. Stuka bombers diving through plump clouds. At the bottom of the page, mis-shaped islands drifting in no-space. On the far left, a little heart-shaped heart, bearing the name of his love in tiny unreadable script.

Jen Webb

COST

National museum of women in the arts

*G-Force Drive, EV Day; Victoria's Secret,
Robin Kahn; Superwoman, Kiki Kogelnik*

They always come free, the old masters,
Though we're centuries out of pocket.
The women we pay to see.

For the masters, we've already paid in
Money, bodies, history. Still, we say
Always, old masters work free.

Thong panties fly from a cannon's mouth
Like comets. Superwoman masks up.
The women we pay to see

Fade, behind bars. In Paris, we've paid
Lives for secrets and taken our change.
Always free, the old masters came,

Always in season, flaneuring
The boulevard, solicitous, soliciting
The women they pay to see

And to paint, not to mention
What they exert on the side. In time,
They always come, the old masters. Free,

Free, the women, in Paris, desire
Masked, put on their paint. Some
Women they pay. To see

Their labor, I proffer my cash,
Consent. In the official museum,
They come free, the old masters. Always,
These women I pay to see.

Katharine Coles

Human looking

Mütter Museum Historic Medical Photographs, 1860-1940

     So much can go wrong. Ulcers or lesions.
     An infestation of worms. Measles, pneumonia, gangrene.
     Some unidentifiable congenital flaw.

Notice how the cursive of this young man's spine
echoes the photographer's signature. This specimen
was acquired in 1877 at a cost of fifty dollars,
on condition that *no questions were to be asked that might
lead to its identification.* I think about the word *its*.
Through this contract, he became the world's
second-tallest skeleton on display.
We are curious.   So much can go wrong.

     Sudden, multiple sarcomas. *Hysterical
     inability to stand or walk. Vestigial tail.*
     A body can be monstrous, shy, mercurial.

This child's head is cradled by adult hands.
It is difficult to discern whether this is for a sense
of scale, the grip tender and subtle,
or if he had to be held down for the image
to be clear enough. I also need
the inscription—*Supernumerary auricle. Idiot.
Incontinence of urine*—to believe there's anything wrong
with him. So, I look again.   So much

     can go wrong. Unstable
     and fatigued, I am liable to fall
     into the belief that I'm not inside these photographs.

R   's hair is slick and neatly combed,
crutches resting against the wall behind him.
He is dressed only in a shirt and vest, pinstripe trousers

folded so as to modestly cover his groin.
I am meant to pay attention to the stump
of his amputated right leg—   the pinched flesh
where the stitches were, hand resting in the vacated space.
It's ok, he's looking into the distance, not the camera.

    How are we meant to look
    at all these injuries sustained from war, from motor vehicles,
    or from carrying wealthy men around on sedan chairs?

And A   's body is still here—
naked and uncannily thin, bones loosely arranged
on an unmade bed. The hard facts
of his ribs and collarbone press up against his skin,
against my eyes. Surely he must be
sleeping, nestled in oblivion. Yet why
is his bed-sheet pulled back to expose him
to the flinches and caresses of my gaze? So

    much can go wrong. Sometimes I might think
    I recognise myself in a patient,
    as if their dignity or torment was mine.

In this photo of a nameless man
with an unspecified disorder of the jaw,
he looks like he may be singing.
Dressed in a tailored three-piece suit and tie,
his expression is composed, almost bored,
yet his mouth is an ecstatic, crooked *O*.
No matter how hard I strain,
I can't hear him.

Andy Jackson

When he charged

head down—index fingers levelled like horns—it was her instinct first to stand her ground and then, at the last moment, to step aside, leaving her brother to thump into the tree, but when her mother—over the years—would say 'poor David', it was she who winced, with nowhere to turn

Paul Munden

The driveway

When they widened our driveway,
the builders ripped out a long-dead gum
and shoved it up by the house.
It stayed there for months,
too big to move, its mesh of branches and roots
riddled with spiders and ants.
We ruined your circular saw
making lean cuts through its thinner limbs,
but the bare trunk remained,
like the carcase of some great animal
that wouldn't rot. In the end,
we slopped petrol all over it, lit a match
and watched old newspapers
writhe and dissemble, like lost souls.
After a while, the trunk grew Gothic black
and fell to ash, became earth,
absence. The next year you got cancer,
and you never came back to us.
Now, there's a dusting of grass where it burned,
a scatter of weeds. The driveway is covered in moss.

John Foulcher

Handwritten

There was no accounting for what we did, spearing jellyfish washed on the foreshore; pushing ourselves on noisy, unsatisfactory swings, feeling our stomachs drop; climbing on backs of trucks. We eventually sundered and you, ringleader for a month, took my early novel and flung it in a creek. Handwritten in green, the words washed away, like inane conversation dissolving in air. Words like thin leaves, flustering restless days.

Paul Hetherington

Cyclone season

Doors bang and windows cry out, the roof is shaking. We cling like children to each other as the waters rise. If we sing very loudly we will not be overwhelmed. So we sing, you looking into my eyes, me with my shifting gaze. If not for you, so people say, I would be at risk of going to the bad. The waters rise, and we give up on the song, and you tread water, holding me. I would give all my fortune to be freed.

Jen Webb

The road to Pac Bo

On a bus I travelled east
into deeper parts of the province
over potted and vexatious roads
past thin fields at the bases of mountains
past wiry dogs and children.
I travelled with babies and women
vomiting into plastic bags—air
pungent with bile.

At *Don Chuong* junction
an old woman posed
for a photograph and cursed
me for not buying from her stall,
and the *xe om* driver came
to charge a price for the pleasures
of twangy country and western
and the vague smell
of coriander and urine as we glided
at one slant and another
in the valley between mountains
on the road to *Pac Bo*.

Shane Strange

My tiny hippopotamus

My tiny hippopotamus, bandog, or lost species, was not mislabelled as a ritual object, unlike the broken combs, cosmetic jars, and other inexplicable mystery discards tweezered from their floodplain or festival-skirted magma tombs. It was labelled as a toy. But for four thousand years nobody has played with it. And when the woman knocked at your side door in the house with no front door and the stillness of a plywood pyramid pressing down abusively gluey inside, you skinned her with one glance and saw you were one blood, you and she, but her people earliest had left the floodplain and the festival-skirted magma tombs where yours wintered and mantraed, deserting much longer after. Much longer after every each day and after the day tomorrow. That is how it is counted. I am six years old plus four and a half thousand years. When she quickly changed the price of her cloth wares and refused to cross your threshold, there were no more toys, only glass, glass for a few thousand years. Your notes danced in her hand and she despised you in her heart. But my reddy-orange toy, which has a happy face, is looking up. I don't mind if you break it. Don't worry about anything. Don't worry. Let's play.

Vahni Capildeo

DIY empire

(the hinge we all hang from)

Trust is getting more expensive. I know
how those people in the Weimar newsreels felt
(except that I don't) but I kid myself I can empathise—
How barrows-ful of cash were required, and yet
insufficient
Never bring a screwdriver to a drill fight, you will only
go down, under-spun, orphaned by light
Every moment so irrevocable, a nail in a nail-gun, and yet

we live our whole lives pretending otherwise,
extenuating

At the going down of the sun, the cashbox must be reconciled   the greasy coins
laid out   we are short   there are dozens of zinc-ed
lips insisting, they will not be silenced, and so I

heave myself into the promotional wheelbarrow, naked but for cheesecloth
artistically arranged   I am moon-like and perfectly bruised, but with
no means of locomotion—perhaps I am hoping to be
grabbed like a dangling handbag, possessed as recompense

for all the unsecured debts, the collapse of this
Rome, everything taken and sullied—OK perhaps just as the first instalment,
one of billions, just enough to cover one tree, one creek, one family
man-handled

Melinda Smith

Questions for the knife

Did you yelp at the blacksmith's hammer?
When you cooled were you cold?
What brass lines your trim?
Whose bone stacked that handle?
How sharp is your edge?
Are you hefty?
Which fish opened their belly to you?
How did you wrest molluscs from the rock?
Did you open your eyes on that black night?
Were you held too tight?
Did you snatch up the sobs?
Are you indifferent to blood?
Were the throats small?

Monica Carroll

YOUTH

So many roads to go

A house. The sun rising and setting. The sparrows' nests you wrecked that afternoon in the barn. Feeding the orphaned lambs, and later weeping over the Sunday roast. When you surfed the Subiaco waves you did not expect that mortality would impress itself on you. From now on it will all be sharks, fast cars, your favourite uncle who loves guns. Try taking it one day at a time. Try not to plan how you'll get from A to Z.

Jen Webb

Bruise

A scribbled-on wall; a broken scooter; five things he badly wanted to say. A man walked sideways towards a garden; a child yelled warfare across the street; doubt was an abstraction needling the body. A doctor prodded a broken finger; words were chewed and tongued in the gripping mouth; flowers blared; the beach was rancorous; a cricket ball banged on the concrete driveway. A penny dropped into a weedy crevice, the girl down the street bit his arm. 'I'll eat you,' she said as he bruised her shoulders with a mistimed lunge.

Paul Hetherington

That photo

I open the envelope, arrange all the pages of my adolescent medical file across the desk, the bed, the floor. If I could see each and every recorded note and image at once—the mapping of heart function, blood pressure, bowel movements, how I described my pain back then—I might find some way to reconcile that time with this. The nurses' handwriting is cryptic, ambiguous. *Light sleeper. Somewhat stooped. Co-operative. Responds to encouragement.* And there I am, twelve, barely flinching in the flash of the camera. Its clinical lens. This poorly photocopied image, all exposure and shadow. A singular person, blurred, nakedly soft. He stands there, unmoving, as I circle him, looking back in time. I catch a foot on the curve of his rib and fall. Chest-deep in this, struggling, I'm sinking, as if awake under anaesthetic, powerless. I can only watch, from within that photo, as a thin and startled boy wanders around the house.

Andy Jackson

Deportment

    1.   Every word
An experiment

Departs. Every
Page transports

Explosions, some
Intentional, others

Grand. Accident
Carries its precedent, posture

Never again will be
This. The head poises

    2.   Atop a body it poses

    3.   A question: what
Contains and does

Self impose
Itself? Balanced

In closing, the books
Ignite inside, they fizz

And spark and send
Up flares. No im-

Position. Or damage
Done. Almost none.

Katharine Coles

Advice poetry

Build networks, not talent.
You will be more successful for who you know than what you do.

♥ everything you see on social media.
You will seem well connected.

Be as cute as a button, or moody with unusual hair.
It is impossible to be both.

Be introduced to someone at least ten times before acknowledging
that you have met them previously.
Forget their name at least ten times more.

Make sure the circles you operate in are closed and self-congratulatory.
They should ideally build their own mythos.

Spend more time documenting what you do instead of doing it.
Leave a good story for archivists of the future.

Suburbs never exist.
They have never existed.
They never will exist.

The environment and the body
are the only safe topics for political expression.
Anything else is 'politics' and beyond the scope of your art.

Write about viscera, incisions, sutures,
splits in organs, arms, torsos and other body parts.
They will represent hurt feelings.
Until those things happen, then they will just hurt.

It is never too late to horn in on a missed opportunity.
But never commit to anything unless you know it will be useful to you.

Someone else can always pay to do the shit you don't want to.

Take opportunities, don't make them for others.

Whatever you do is more important.

Expect, but never give, compliments.

To lend anything gravitas, finish it with 'poetry'.

Shane Strange

The band

We worshipped Ron McLaughlin—
Paul McCartney, bass guitar. The acned,
gangling singer, John (something, I don't know)
would strut and prance, the microphone's
electric lead knotting him to Donny,
twitching Jimi Hendrix, leadening guitar.
The drummer, Garrie, was the clown,
as every drummer is. . . Now they're drowned
in memory, though Ron McLaughlin
floats there still, a buoy among the waves.
Long-haired, dark-eyed and dangerous,
he knew the things you don't let slip,
how mystery beguiles. . . Once,
when school was nearly done, I watched
them at a party, staking out a stage
in someone else's house. Perching
by the door with Tommy and with Dale,
I heard them tuning up. Then Ron McLaughlin
smiled at us, pushing past and leaving,
his arm around the busty girl
who tinted us with just a glance.
Tommy winked and whispered *He is gunna
fuck her stupid.* We nodded knowingly,
promise and experience divided
by a sound. Standing there in silence,
pretending we were cool, we thought
of Ron McLaughlin fingering the nameless
girl, naked in her room. They were back
in minutes, though, with whiskey for the band.
Sober and alone, we slipped outside
and left. The music crashed and roared.

John Foulcher

Their father still refused

to take out the trees—five eucalypts screening the house, sole survivors among the white picket fences and open lawns—while opposite, a huge red river gum towered over the slope of scrub where every ball would bounce away, lost... and you liked that house—its modern brick and blue tiled roof—for all its cramped simplicity, and will not forget the afternoon you sat there after school, low sun fanning deep shadows through the trees, knowing that time would never again be wholly yours

Paul Munden

As we rolled out the tape measure tongue—at a mark between 40 and 50 centimetres—an astounding fact came to be known

Little sister saved us all: the maidens, the mule and the monster: all spared from the spell of premeditated murder. The monster, in rage, claimed a turtle of rock and named out the clouds.

It was a test.

There is a peacock, growled the beast.
Yes, said little sister, I see it.
An ox, avowed the deformity.
Yes, she repeated.
Dragon.
Yes. Yes.
The monster's broken eggs were healed. Shell cracks mended. Yoke membrane treated. He was planning to eat us but felt suddenly full.

Monica Carroll

every each day best

bring up the girl without pink
says princess daddy
eat rhoticity chicken
resist transgressive dickery

Vahni Capildeo

Interrupting the bread-making

The frost has woken her early
She pads into the freezing kitchen
in her hand-me-down quilted dressing-gown
sniffing the yeasty air
She is discovering for the first time
her father's secret early morning life
Almost younger than words,
she can only stroke solemnly
the ears of the knitted rabbit
cradled in her arm
and watch
as he claps flour from his grey hands
wrenches open the door of the pot-bellied stove,
prods a roaring orange monster mouth
with a long metal wand
There are nuggets inside, blurred with flame
They flare and settle, the mouth
spits little pellets of grey
onto the hearthstone
like biscuit crumbs, like bread crumbs
She reaches for them, too late
the air is full of loud
and from that moment
the word *No* is black and orange and ash,
is the sound of skin sizzling,
is the texture of a puckered fingertip,
and *Don't touch* somehow smells
like coking coal and yeast and father, and
curiosity, stubbornness, defiance,
sting like bare feet on a winter morning,
chafe like coarse wool
dig like a dressing gown cord
pink, frayed, tied too tight—

a cord which is not umbilical
but which is, nevertheless
a species of tether

Melinda Smith

N O T E S

'Introduction', Paul Munden and Shane Strange, p iii
    None of the poets were aware of our further, slightly mischievous conceit—forming an additional abstraction from the initial letters of the chosen set.

'Through eye-gate, and ear-gate into the city of child-soul', Shane Strange p 66
    Altered from text found in *With the Children on Sundays* by Sylvanus Stall.

'The road to *Pac Bo*', Shane Strange, p 122
    Pac Bo is the name of the remote place on the border of China where Ho Chi Minh, after four decades in exile, crossed back into Vietnam.
    A *xe om* is a motorbike taxi.

'Marks', Melinda Smith, p 101
    Phrases in italics are quotes from Bligh, William, MS 5393-Notebook and list of mutineers, 1789 [manuscript]./Item 2, p 1, held in the National Library of Australia and accessible here: https://nla.gov.au/nla.obj-233730330/view

'DIY empire', Melinda Smith, p 124
    This poem is an acrostic on the phrase 'the hinge we all hang from', from the last line of Angela Gardner's poem, 'three fragments'.

'Deportment', Katharine Coles, p 132
    After Paul Strand, *Anna Attinga Frafra, Accra, Ghana*. Picture of a teenage girl balancing books on her head.

The following poems have been previously published:

'That photo', Andy Jackson, was first published the *Time anthology of micro-lit* (ed. Cassandra Atherton, Spineless Wonders, 2018); 'No relief maps', Andy Jackson, was exhibited as a response to a digital artwork, and was published in the accompanying book, Return Flight Edition 2.0, (ed. Megan Anderson, *Going Down Swinging*, 2018) - http://www.blindside.org.au/return-flight-melchc; 'With daily practice' and 'Road Closed', Paul Munden, were first published in States of Poetry ACT, Series Three (ed. Jen Webb), *Australian Book Review;* 'Their father still refused', Paul Munden, was first published in *The Stony Thursday Book*, No. 16 (ed. Nessa O'Mahony).

BIOGRAPHIES

MONICA CARROLL used to hold the hose for the concrete mixer but now she writes. If you like creepy poetry read her book *Isolator* (Recent Work Press, 2017). Or find her slightly less creepy academic essays listed on monicacarroll.com.au.

VAHNI CAPILDEO's books include *Venus as a Bear* (Forward Poetry Prizes Best Collection shortlist; Poetry Book Society Summer Choice), *Measures of Expatriation* (Forward Poetry Prizes Best Collection award; TS Eliot Prize nomination) and *Utter*. Capildeo studied Old Norse and translation theory, and has worked in academia, lexicography, and culture for development. They enjoy non-traditional theatre-making and writing non-fiction. Capildeo is a traditional masquerader who has become Pierrot Grenade and the Midnight Robber, and belongs to Belmont Exotic Stylish Sailors. Capildeo's homes are in Scotland and Trinidad. They are the Douglas Caster Cultural Fellow in Poetry at the University of Leeds.

KATHARINE COLES' forthcoming books are a memoir, *Look Both Ways* (Turtle Point Press, 2018); and a collection of poems, *Wayward* (Red Hen Press, 2019). She has received awards from the National Endowment for the Arts, the National Science Foundation, and the National Endowment for the Humanities (all USA), as well as from the Guggenheim Foundation. She is a Distinguished Professor of English at the University of Utah.

JOHN FOULCHER has written 11 books of poetry, most recently *101 Poems* (Pitt Street Poetry, 2015), a selection from his previous books, and *A Casual Penance* (Pitt Street Poetry, 2017). His work has appeared in national magazines and anthologies for over thirty years. In 2010-11 he was the Literature Board's resident at the Keesing Studio in Paris; his collection, *The Sunset Assumption* (Pitt Street Poetry, 2012) reflects on that experience. His poetry was set for study on the NSW Higher School Certificate syllabus for an extended period of time. He lives in Canberra.

PAUL HETHERINGTON has published 13 collections of poetry and prose poetry including, most recently, *Moonlight on Oleander: Prose Poems*. He won the 2014 Western Australian Premier's Book Award (poetry) and was shortlisted for the 2017 Kenneth Slessor Prize for Poetry, the 2018 international *Aesthetica* Creative Writing Competition (poetry) and the 2018 Grieve Writing Competition (poetry). He heads the International Poetry Studies Institute (IPSI) in the Faculty of Arts and Design at the University of Canberra where he is also Professor of Writing. With Cassandra Atherton he is writing a scholarly study of the prose poem for Princeton University Press.

ANDY JACKSON has featured at literary events and arts festivals in Australia, India, USA and Ireland, and his poems have been selected for five of the last six annual editions of *The Best Australian Poems*. Andy's most recent collection, *Music our bodies can't hold* (Hunter Publishers, 2017), consists of portrait poems of other people with Marfan Syndrome.

PAUL MUNDEN has published five poetry collections, most recently *Chromatic* (UWA Publishing, 2017). He was director of Poetry on the Move, 2015-17, and director of the UK's National Association of Writers in Education, 1994-2018. He has worked as conference poet for the British Council, reader for Stanley Kubrick, and script editor for GSP Studios. He is co-editor with Nessa O'Mahony of *Metamorphic: 21st century poets respond to Ovid* (Recent Work Press, 2017), and editor of *Strange Cargo: Five Australian Poets* (Smith|Doorstop, 2017).

MELINDA SMITH is the author of six books of poetry, most recently *Goodbye, Cruel* (Pitt Street Poetry, 2017). She won the 2014 Prime Minister's Literary Award for *Drag down to unlock or place an emergency call* and her work has been widely anthologised and translated into multiple languages. She is based in the ACT and is a former poetry editor of the *Canberra Times*.

SHANE STRANGE is a Teaching Fellow in Creative Writing at the University of Canberra. His writing has been published widely in Australia. In 2010, he was an Asialink Literature fellow. He is also a publisher and editor at Recent Work Press, a poetry press based in Canberra, Australia.

JEN WEBB is director of the Centre for Creative and Cultural Research, and researches the role of art in society. The ACT editor of *Australian Book Review*'s States of Poetry annual anthology and, with Paul Hetherington, of the English/Mandarin bilingual anthology *Open Windows: Contemporary Australian Poetry*, she is also author of several poetry collections and of collaborative artist books. Her most recent poetry collection is *Moving Targets* (Recent Work Press, 2018). Jen is Distinguished Professor of Creative Practice at the University of Canberra.

2018 Editions
The Uncommon Feast **Eileen Chong**
Inlandia **Kerry Nelson**
Peripheral Vision **Martin Dolan**
The Love of the Sun **Matt Hetherington**
Moving Targets **Jen Webb**
Things I Have Thought to Tell You Since I Saw You Last **Penelope Layland**
The Many Uses of Mint **Ravi Shankar**
Abstractions **Various**

2017 Editions
A Song, the World to Come **Miranda Lello**
Cities: Ten Poets, Ten Cities **Various**
The Bulmer Murder **Paul Munden**
Dew and Broken Glass **Penny Drysdale**
Members Only **Melinda Smith** and **Caren Florance**
the future, un-imagine **Angela Gardner** and **Caren Florance**
Proof **Maggie Shapley**
Black Tulips **Moya Pacey**
Soap **Charlotte Guest**
Isolator **Monica Carroll**
Ikaros **Paul Hetherington**
Work & Play **Owen Bullock**

all titles available from
www.recentworkpress.com

www.ingramcontent.com/pod-product-compliance
Ingram Content Group UK Ltd.
Pitfield, Milton Keynes, MK11 3LW, UK
UKHW041302180426
11947UKWH00009B/636